DATE DUE

OCT 0 5 2011		
GAYLORD		PRINTED IN U.S.A.

Digging for Answers

ISBN 0-9743137-2-6

Published by Alpine Archaeological Consultants, Inc.
P.O. Box 2075
Montrose, CO 81402

Design: Marlise Reed
Unless otherwise credited, illustrations by: Marlise Reed and Eric Carlson
Map: Stephanie Dudash

Front Cover: Hunting Antelope, Marlise Reed

Digging for Answers

Prehistoric Archaeology
in Northwestern Colorado

by Marlise Reed

Alpine Archaeological Consultants, Inc., Publisher

Acknowledgments

This book is part of the archaeological programs conducted by Alpine Archaeological Consultants, Inc. (Alpine) and Metcalf Archaeological Consultants, Inc. (MAC) for Wyoming Interstate Company's Piceance Basin Expansion pipeline and the Rockies Express pipeline. The project consists of two natural gas pipelines built mostly next to each other in Rio Blanco and Moffat counties, Colorado. The archaeological programs included identifying historic and prehistoric sites along the pipeline corridor and conducting archaeological excavations at sites most likely to answer important research questions.

A number of agencies and individuals contributed to the successful completion of the archaeological investigations, to whom Alpine and MAC are grateful. The lead government agency for the two pipeline projects was the Federal Energy Regulatory Commission; Ms Laurie Boros was that agency's assigned archaeologist. The Bureau of Land Management played a key role in project management, especially Colorado State Archaeologist Dan Haas, White River Field Office archaeologist Michael Selle, and Little Snake Field Office Archaeologist Robyn Morris. The Colorado State Historic Preservation Office also oversaw the project.

MAC and Alpine thank the landowners who allowed archaeological excavations to take place on their land: Sterling Cook Living Trust & Mary Cook Living Trust, Marion Lake Culbertson and Bill Lake, Sam and Georgia McIntyre, John Raftopolis and Steve Raftopolis, Bruce and Ellen Strickler, Nottingham Land & Livestock, Samuel and Edna Kelsall, and Visintainer Sheep Company, as well as the State of Colorado Division of Wildlife and Colorado State Land Board.

Contents

"Every archaeologist knows in his heart why he digs. He digs... that the dead may live again, that what is past may not be forever lost, that something may be salvaged from the wrack of ages, that the past may color the present and give heart to the future."

-T. Geoffrey Bibby
The Testimony of the Spade

Landscape in northwestern Colorado project region

Introduction

Around 13,000 years ago, people first settled in Colorado. These prehistoric groups followed herds of big game throughout the year, making shelters and camps as they went. They created tools and weapons from the rocks and materials in their environment, collected edible plants, and stored food for the lean winter months. As the centuries passed, people continued moving and settling, leaving traces of their day-to-day lives on the landscape. These traces include pieces of pottery, arrowheads, and flakes from making stone tools. Their buried fire pits give clues about what kinds of food they were eating and how long ago the sites were used. Archaeologists use all of the information they discover to put together a picture of how the prehistoric inhabitants of this area lived and what their culture may have been like.

This book shares the results of the archaeological investigations conducted in northwestern Colorado by Alpine Archaeological Consultants, Inc. and Metcalf Archaeological Consultants, Inc. Substantial archaeological excavations were completed, providing many answers about the prehistoric peoples who lived here for thousands of years. Historic archaeology is part of archaeological work as well; however, this book focuses on prehistoric archaeology to reflect the findings of the project.

How are prehistoric sites protected by law?

In the United States, numerous State and Federal laws protect archaeological sites. The purpose of these laws is to secure sites and artifacts on public and Indian lands for present and future generations of Americans. The Archaeological Resources Protection Act, for example, makes it a felony to loot or damage sites on public or Indian lands. Archaeologists who want to study these sites must first obtain a permit from the government.

Federal agencies that build, fund, or authorize projects are required by the National Historic Preservation Act to consider the effects of their actions on important archaeological sites and historic buildings. They must identify historic properties, evaluate their significance, determine how they will be affected by the projects, and decide on measures to lessen any adverse effects. Mitigation measures for prehistoric sites generally include scientific excavation and analysis, public interpretation, and the long-term care of the resulting collections and records so that these will be available for future research.

Archaeological sites are an irreplaceable part of our nation's heritage. By protecting them we can preserve them for future generations.

This archaeology project and book were jointly funded by the Rockies Express Pipeline LLC (REX) and the Wyoming Interstate Company (WIC) in preparation for building two pipelines through Rio Blanco and Moffat counties in Colorado.

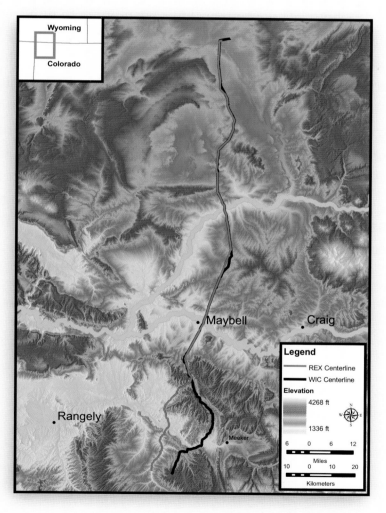

Map showing project area in northwestern Colorado

Why do archaeology?

Archaeology is a way of learning about life in the past by studying the places where people lived and the objects that they left behind. The Americas have been home to hundreds of cultures for over 13,000 years. Archaeological research focuses on items left behind during people's activities, including fragments of pottery vessels, food remains, firepits, human remains, stone tools, or evidence left from the construction of dwellings. Many other aspects of the culture of prehistoric peoples are not preserved in the archaeological record, however. Their beliefs and behaviors are difficult to decipher from physical materials. Prehistoric languages remain unknown, as the Native American groups in the western U.S. had no known writing system.

Archaeologists recover and analyze the material and biological remains of past cultures in hopes of understanding the social systems, traditions, and practices that were the way of life for prehistoric and historic peoples. The remains of these cultures, such as sites, artifacts, and structures, are a part of our nation's heritage.

What do archaeologists do?

Archaeologists do their work in several stages. The first stage consists of "survey." Surveying involves walking the land that might be disturbed by a proposed project to find any sites visible on the ground surface. A site is any location where past human activities can be identified. Once located, all sites are mapped, photographed, and recorded.

Recording identifies sites that are especially important; efforts are often made to avoid important sites, if possible.

The second stage of the archaeological project is excavation. Excavation is the exposure, processing, and documenting of archaeological remains in the field. Collected materials are then analyzed by archaeologists in the laboratory to help interpret past physical and social systems.

The results from the analysis are written up in reports to share the data gathered. Books such as this one are created to share the information with the public. Artifacts collected during the excavation stage are carefully catalogued and, if collected on public lands, curated at a museum. The artifacts are available for future research and public education.

Excavation of a basin house in northwestern Colorado

Do archaeologists really dig with brushes and dental picks?

Occasionally fine tools like dental picks and brushes are used during excavations to perform delicate tasks. Artifacts like bone and other easily damaged materials need to be handled with care as not to damage them during excavation.

Not all work is done with such specialized tools. Heavy machinery like backhoes can be used if a site is deeply buried. Shovels and trowels are the tools most commonly used to unearth artifacts and features such as hearths. Excavations are usually done on a tight schedule before construction work. These larger tools allow archaeologists to work quickly while still being careful enough to preserve any artifacts found.

Carefully excavating animal bones

What happens to the artifacts that archaeologists excavate?

It depends upon where the artifacts were found. If they were excavated on private land, they belong to the landowner. The landowner can choose to donate the artifacts to a museum, where they can be displayed and made available for research.

If the artifacts were excavated on public land, the pieces are carefully recorded and cared for in a qualified museum. None of the artifacts are kept by the archaeology companies. All artifacts are analyzed by archaeologists before they are returned to landowners or placed in a museum. This information helps archaeologists understand how the prehistoric peoples lived.

Archaeologist studying artifacts in the lab. All collected artifacts are catalogued and analyzed before being returned or placed in a museum.

Do archaeologists dig dinosaur bones?

Archaeologists do not dig dinosaur bones--they study only the human past. Scientists who study dinosaur bones (or fossils) are called paleontologists. The last of the dinosaurs died out about 65 million years ago. Our earliest hominid (human-like) ancestors did not appear until about 5 million years ago. For the entire time that people have been around, dinosaurs have been extinct. Their fossils help paleontologists study the history of life on earth, but dinosaur bones do not help archaeologists understand human prehistory.

Archaeologists who specialize in studying animal bones study zooarchaeology, which means "the archaeology of animals." Zooarchaeologists look at the relationships between people and animals in the past. They analyze bones found in early human settlements to see what people were hunting and eating. Both paleontologists and archaeologists excavate and study animal bones, but only paleontologists study dinosaurs.

When did people first appear in northwestern Colorado?

Human occupation of northwestern Colorado began approximately 13,000 years ago at the beginning of the Paleoindian era. This era was the period between 11,500 and 6400 B.C. During this time, prehistoric people had access to plants and some animals that are now extinct. Human population levels were low and animal populations were high, making big game an important and stable source of food. When animal resources were depleted in an area, people simply moved on to a new location. As human populations increased, their mobile lifestyle was gradually replaced by a more settled and localized one.

What did they eat?

Prehistoric people in much of northwestern Colorado were hunters and gatherers who had to spend much of their time procuring food. They were very mobile, leaving an area when food resources became depleted. As herds of animals moved with the seasons, the people would follow. Plants and seeds were gathered all through the growing season and were an important source of food. During the cold season, people would eat the foods that they had stored earlier in the year. These would include dried meat, berries, nuts, and seeds.

Most of the animals in their environment were a source of food for prehistoric people. These included antelope, deer, bison, rabbit, ground squirrel, lizards, fish, birds, and even grasshoppers and Mormon crickets. Bison probably played a smaller role in their diet because they were not as plentiful in this region compared to other portions of the plains.

Plants provided a large percentage of the calories people consumed. The inhabitants of northwestern Colorado had access to acorns, seeds from sunflowers, cattail pollen and roots, prickly pear cactus, grass seeds, pinyon nuts, pigweed, and goosefoot plants. These were collected as they came into season.

Did they grow crops?

In northwestern Colorado, the people of the Formative era moved so frequently that plant cultivation likely played only a small part in their way of life. There is some evidence that they may have planted and harvested pigweed and goosefoot. Pigweed and goosefoot are similar plants that were an important part of their diet. They are weedy plants that produce lots of small seeds that can be eaten, stored, and ground into meal. The leaves can be eaten as greens.

Goosefoot and pigweed usually grow in wet zones near creeks, but can be grown elsewhere if watered and tended. When archaeologists find evidence of these plants growing far from water, it is likely that they were planted there by people who could tend and water them. As they were domesticated, the amount of seeds on the plant increased and the seed coats became thinner. These are clues that plant analysts look for to indicate that the plant was cultivated by prehistoric people. It is not certain whether these plants were domesticated in this region at the time, but pigweed and goosefoot played an important part in their diet.

Women gathering Indian ricegrass,
a grass with large, plentiful seeds that
was a staple of their diet.

Skinning bison after a hun
Women were likely the one
who performed this task.

Fires were used for cooking many of their foods. Meats were roasted on spits above the flames. Rock-lined pits were used for roasting tubers, roots and meats. Jerking was an important way of preparing meats because jerky could be stored for long periods of time. Racks to dry the meat were likely made of branches.

Many of their foods were prepared into stews. Their baskets were woven tightly and coated with pitch, making them waterproof and usable as cooking vessels. Heated rocks were put into the baskets to boil the contents. The ingredients in the stews varied through the year, often using a base of flour made from seeds. Greens, seasonings, meat, and any other food would have been included as well.

"Desert fruitcake" is a type of food prepared from dried berries, meat, seeds, and sometimes grasshoppers. The ingredients were formed into loaves and cooked on heated flat stones. This food was a good source of protein and calories and could be stored for future use.

How do archaeologists determine the age of sites?

Various methods are used to date sites. Some methods are more accurate than others, and archaeologists have a greater range of dating methods now than they did many years ago. Relative dating gives an estimated age of an artifact, while absolute dating gives a more exact number.

Relative dating consists of measuring natural processes that can be observed. An example of this is stratigraphy, which measures the different layers of rock, sediments, and soils in the ground. We know that objects closer to the surface are almost always more recent than objects buried under deep layers of dirt.

Excavated fire pit several feet below the surface

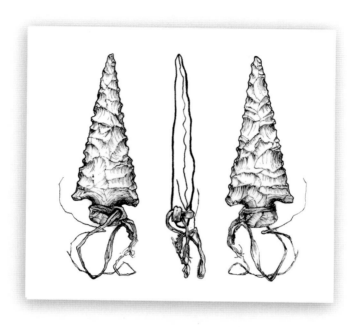

Another type of relative dating is cross-dating. Artifacts from the site are compared to artifacts of known age. Styles and techniques of creating objects change over time, making it possible to date pottery, projectile points, and many other artifacts this way.

Obsidian hydration is an absolute dating method used to date artifacts made from obsidian. Obsidian is a volcanic glass that forms during volcanic eruptions and was used for making stone tools. This material slowly absorbs water from the environment at a relatively consistent rate. As time goes on, it absorbs more and more water, forming a hydration band from the surface inward. This band can be measured to tell how long ago the obsidian was broken to form a tool. A small sample of obsidian is cut from the artifact for dating.

Absolute dating provides more accurate dates by using scientific tests done on materials collected in the field. Types of absolute dating methods commonly used by archaeologists are tree-ring dating, radiocarbon dating, and thermoluminescence dating.

Tree-ring dating is based on patterning of growth rings. Annual changes in available water affects growth patterns to create a history of the tree, giving information about what time in history the tree died. Because people find and use old wood, this method of dating does not always show the actual date of the site, but the date that the tree died.

Radiocarbon dating can date any material that was once living. This includes bone, charcoal or other charred plant material, and even protein residue found on the edge of projectile points. This method is based on the fact that all living things contain a type of carbon isotope, Carbon-14 (^{14}C), which is mildly radioactive. This isotope decays at a set rate over time. By measuring how much ^{14}C remains in the material, scientists are able to estimate how long ago it died. This process can only measure up to 50,000 years, at which point all of the ^{14}C has disappeared. Samples of charcoal from many of the hearths on this project were dated using this method.

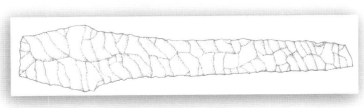

Another type of dating that can be done is thermoluminescence dating. This method is used mainly to date ceramic artifacts. When a ceramic artifact is fired, ions trapped in the material excape. Over time, the ceramic reabsorbs radiation that is naturally present in the environment. The measure of the radiation present in the ceramic provides the time frame for this type of dating. The thermoluminescence method can be used to date artifacts for materials as far back as 100,000 years. Because pottery was a material that was easily broken and constantly replenished, it is a good indicator of when people were actually occupying a site.

The locations of all artifacts collected by archaeologists are carefully recorded. When the date of some artifacts are learned through these dating methods, other artifacts in the site can be interpreted as well. All of these methods except tree-ring dating were used in the analysis of this project. Most of the artifacts found dated to the Archaic period (around 6,400 to 200 B.C.).

What were their houses like?

Most prehistoric houses in northwestern Colorado are called "basin houses" by archaeologists. Because most of the material used to make the houses has decomposed, they look like saucer-shaped depressions or floors. The house is believed to have been a conically shaped structure with a wooden pole frame, over which materials like bark, hides, or tree boughs were placed. The floors may have been partly covered with mats, stripped bark, or grasses. A fire pit inside the house would have allowed for cooking indoors as well as heating the dwelling. Some houses contained floor pits thought to have been used for storage.

Artist's reconstruction of a basin house. Cut-away on right shows inside view.

Artist's rendition of a wikiup

During the summer, houses were less substantial. They may have been as simple as a sunshade or a "wickiup," which are both made from branches and brush. These houses were formed with a frame of wooden poles and covered with branches or hides. Because structures made of wood are less likely to be preserved, most of the housing structures found by archaeologists are the more permanent winter residences. Standing wikiups have been found in northwestern Colorado.

What kind of tools did they use?

The prehistoric people used a variety of different tools. Many of these were made out of sandstone, river cobbles, quartzite, or chert. Chert and quartzite are fine-grained rocks that can be flaked into tools with sharp edges. Their grinding tools consisted of a large slab of rock for the metate and a smaller, hand-held rock for the mano. These were chosen based on their shape and texture and little work was done to make them usable as tools.

Above; A mano and metate found under a tree. The mano has worn a basin into the metate.

Left; A broken drill point. The top of the drill would have extended into a sharp point.

More work went into creating projectile points, knives, and scrapers. These tools were usually made from chert, but sometimes obsidian was found or acquired through trade. This material was turned into sharp points by flint-knapping, the practice of striking the rock with a hammerstone or an antler to break off small flakes. The piece would be worked into the shape that the person desired. These sharp tools were useful as knives, scrapers, and projectile points. They made drills using a stone tip and a small hand-held bow to spin the drill. This was used to drill holes in bone and shell to make beads.

Flint-knapping

Projectile points

Some pieces of chert show signs of heat-treatment of the raw material, which changes the crystalline structure of the rock and improves the knapping quality.

Another type of tool used by prehistoric people was a piece of stone used to smooth the shaft of arrows. A rock the size of a person's palm was used for this task, and the repetition of the work left a straight groove across the stone.

Scrapers made from chert

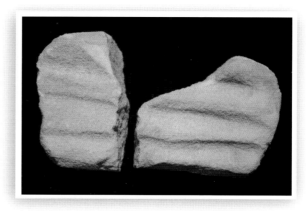

Broken tool used to smooth arrow shafts

The edges of this hammerstone show wear from striking objects.

Other tools included hammerstones, a rock used to hammer other objects. Some tools were multi-purpose tools and could be used for a variety of tasks. Based on the wear on their manos and metates, it is apparent that people used these tools until they broke or were too worn out to work. If a projectile point broke, they sometimes were able to rework the edges and make another usable tool out of it.

Long knife

What tools did they use to grind seeds?

Handstones, called manos, were used to grind seeds against a larger slab of rock called a metate. The mano was small enough to be held in one hand and was moved across seeds or other foods on the metate. The slab metate was a larger, heavier stone that would rest on the ground. The rough surfaces of the two stones together turned the seeds into ground meal or flour. These tools were used so often that an indentation in the metate would develop, forming a basin. The bottom of the mano would become flat and smooth after consistent use. These patterns of wear are what archaeologists look for to see if stones have been used as milling tools.

Mano and slab metate

Grinding stones made it possible for people to use foods like small hard seeds. Dried or parched seeds store longer than fresh or soaked seeds, but are not very versatile for cooking without being ground. Foods made from ground seeds and grains cook faster, using less cooking fuel. A greater variety of items could be made from the processed seeds. One drawback to this type of milling is that the wear on the stones left small amounts of sand and rock fragments in the ground meal. After years, the sand would cause people's teeth to become worn.

What is an atlatl?

An atlatl is a tool used to throw long darts or spears. This tool gave the prehistoric people an advantage in hunting by increasing the distance and speeds at which their darts could be thrown.

The atlatl is a stick about 2 feet long with a handgrip at one end and a spur at the other. The spur is a point that fits in to a cavity at the back of a four-to-six foot dart. The dart is similar to a large arrow, with a long flexible shaft and a projectile point attached to the tip. To use the atlatl, the dart is suspended parallel to the board and held by the tips of the fingers at the handgrip. The thrower launches the dart with a sweeping arm and wrist motion similar to a tennis serve.

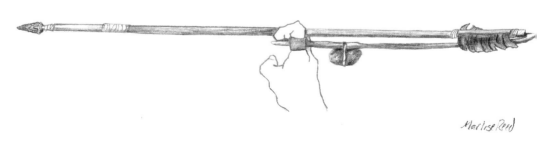

Eric Carlson

The atlatl allows the hunter to throw a dart much farther than he could by hand. The tool produces leverage to achieve greater velocity in the throw, which increases the speed and distance the dart can be thrown. The range of a dart thrown by an atlatl can exceed the distance of a football field and can achieve speeds of over 90 miles per hour. However, the atlatl is most accurate at distances of 60 feet or less.

Why did the bow and arrow replace the atlatl?

The bow and arrow started to replace the atlatl about 1,600 years ago. Although the atlatl had its advantages, such as delivering over twice the force upon impact as an arrow, it also had its drawbacks. A hunter using the spear thrower needed more room to launch and throw than a hunter with a bow needed to shoot the arrow. The projectiles for the atlatl were larger and carried by hand, which limited the amount of darts a hunter could carry to only five or six. Arrows, being smaller and lighter weight, could be carried in a quiver holding as many as twenty arrows.

The larger darts for the atlatl were good for hunting large game, but the bow and arrow had more versatility in hunting different types and sizes of animals.

The arrow is also more accurate than the atlatl at close ranges. About 1,600 years ago populations were increasing. The ability to hunt large and small animals with an arrow was important and permitted use of a wider range of animals for food. Atlatls were better for hunting large game than for hunting smaller animals like rabbits. The bow and arrow could be used for hunting individually, but the atlatl was more commonly used by groups hunting together. This shift also led to the bow being favored over the spear thrower.

Archaeologists can tell the difference between projectile points used for the atlatl and the bow and arrow based on the size of the point. Arrowheads are smaller than the points used on the darts for the atlatl. Once the bow and arrow was introduced, it became more widely used than the atlatl and its use spread to all groups.

Dart point and arrowhead

Hunting antelope with bow and arrow

33

What did they wear?

The exact type and style of clothing worn by prehistoric people is mostly unknown because the materials they were made from disintegrated over time. Remains of some items of clothing have been found in protected caves and overhangs. Based on the materials available to them and the few clothing artifacts that have been found, it is likely that they made clothing out of leather, furs, and bark. The prehistoric people knew how to weave and make rope by twisting grasses or bark strips together. Fragments of fur blankets that were likely used as shoulder blankets have been found in caves in Utah. Pieces of rabbit furs were twisted in a way that left the fur on the outside and were then woven together into a garment. Fur shoulder blankets and wraps would have been used during the cold seasons.

Men probably wore hide breechcloths and leggings while the women probably made dresses from hides. In summer, women may have worn skirts made from bark. Children likely wore very little clothing in warm seasons. Moccasins were used for footwear, made from leather sewn together by punching holes in the hide with an awl and then lacing sinew through to connect the pieces. During winter, they would line their moccasins with bark for added insulation. Decorative items like headdresses and necklaces were worn as well, though some of them may have been ceremonial rather than every day wear.

*Historic photo showing a man
wearing a woven rabbit skin
robe and leather leggings*

Although this woman is from a tribe in northern California, her rabbit skin robe is a good example of a type of weaving likely done by the prehistoric people of northern Colorado as well.

What kind of weaving did people do?

Prehistoric people used materials such as sagebrush bark and cattails to weave a variety of items like baskets, seed beaters, fur blankets, and mats for floors. They did not use looms for weaving, but were able to create many useful items by twining and weaving different materials. Rabbit skin blankets were made by cutting a skin into a long continuous strip and then twisted upon itself until it was furry on all sides. The strips were then twined together with buckskin string to make a blanket. These were used for sleeping and as shoulder blankets in the winter. Seed beaters were a woven paddle used to remove the hulls from grass seeds and grains.

Example of coiled basket weaving. Split fibers were coiled around a central rod then stitched together.

36

Did prehistoric peoples have jewelery?

Handmade beads were used as jewelry for ornamentation by prehistoric people. The beads were made of stone, bone, or shell, and carved into a round shape with a hole drilled in the center. Beads would have been strung onto necklaces or sewn onto clothing.

Some shell beads have been found in northwestern Colorado that show trade between the people of this region and coastal tribes. These beads were made from a type of shell found in the Gulf of California, showing that these items were valuable enough to carry over long distances. Beads were treasured because they were attractive, exotic, and durable as well as a valuable trade item.

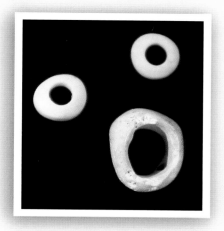

Three beads found in project area. The top two are made from shell. The larger bead is made from bone.

What kind of baskets did they make?

Baskets were important items for the prehistoric people. Various shapes and sizes were made depending on intended use. Some baskets were waterproof and could be used for cooking. These baskets were woven tightly, then waterproofed by coating the basket with heated pine pitch to seal any spaces. Heated rocks were added to the liquid in the basket until the contents were boiling. Burden baskets were large cone-shaped baskets used when gathering plants and seeds. A strap that could be worn around the forehead was connected to the basket's rim, making it possible to carry items on the back without hands. Basketry remains are rarely found by archaeologists unless they have been protected from the elements in a cave or overhang.

A MONO HOME

This historic photo shows a wikiup and burden baskets similar in style to the summer housing and baskets that were used in northwestern Colorado.

Did they use pottery?

People began making pottery around 700 A.D. during the Formative era. Pot sherds found in the project area were made by the early Ute and Shoshone inhabitants of the region. Stylistic differences can be seen between the ceramics of the two groups. The Ute pottery, more common in northwestern Colorado, was formed into vessels with slightly flaring rims and pointed or round bases. The Shoshone pottery usually had a flat base and edges that flared out, similar in shape to a flower pot. This group lived further north in the area that is now southern Wyoming.

The pottery from these regions is called "brown ware," referring to the colors of the clay and the variations in color caused by firing. Most pieces range from brownish-red to brownish-black. The pieces were fired at low heat, likely in small pits covered with brush. The pottery was not heavily decorated. This shows that it was a functional object

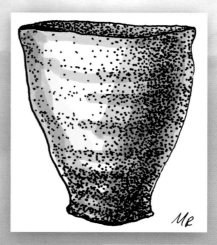

Shoshone-style pot

rather than an object to express identity or group affiliation. Several of the pot sherds found in this region have markings on them from fingernail indentations. These impressions are characteristic of Ute pottery.

The blackening and soot found on the exterior side of the sherds shows that the vessels were likely used in fires for cooking. The open, wide-mouthed shape of these pots is consistent with vessels used for boiling liquids rather than storage. Using pottery for cooking had the advantage that it was less labor intensive to place a pot in the fire than to cook with baskets. Boiling water in a basket required heated stones to be frequently added, but a pot needed minimal supervision. Pottery was also used for storage and transport.

*Ceramic pot sherd showing
fingernail indentation*

What can prehistoric fire pits tell us about the past?

Prehistoric fire pits can give a lot of interesting information about a site. The charcoal from the fire pits is sent off for radiocarbon dating, a scientific test that tells the date of the site. Analyzing the charcoal also shows what type of fuel was being burned, giving the archaeologist an idea of what types of shrubs or trees were growing in the area at the time. In this region, sagebrush was the main fuel used. Rocks from the feature can be tested for protein or starch residue and plant remains, showing what types of food were being cooked in the pits. Animal bones found in the fire pit indicate what types of meat the prehistoric people were eating. Fire pits probably had a range of functions, including simple heating, cooking, roasting, and heating stones to boil water.

Rock-lined fire pit

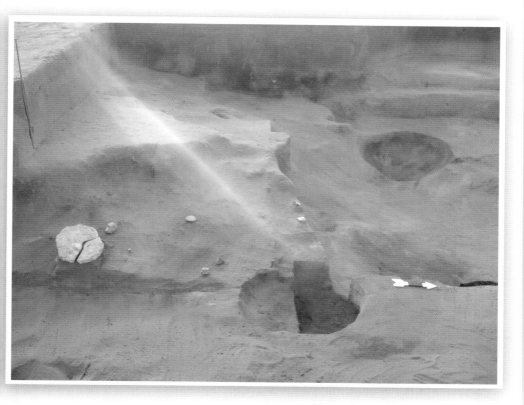

Excavated basin house with interior hearths

Fire pits can also give clues to what length of time the site was occupied. A site that was going to be lived in for longer periods of time would have had more complex, well-built features than a site that was only used for a short time.

The different sizes and depths of fire pits indicate their original use. Deep, rock-lined pits were used for roasting meat, roots, and tubers. These required more construction than simple fire pits. Shallow, smaller pits were likely used for heating, waste disposal, and cooking.

What did they use to store things?

Many of the basin houses had multiple pits built into the floor, similar to the fire pits, but used for storage. Storage pits were used to cache tools or store food. Sites that were occupied during the cold months had more features associated with storage than did summer sites. Food storage was important to get people through the lean winters.

Tools were sometimes stored for later use. Prehistoric people moved frequently and had to carry all of their belongings, so it saved energy to leave some things behind. Objects made from stone, like manos and metates, were heavy and difficult to carry while traveling. They would be left at a site where people knew they would return. Some tools and materials were related to work done during specific times of year, so it made sense to leave these objects near the winter or summer camp where they would be used.

Measuring an obsidian point

*Broken arrowhead
with penny for scale*

How do projectile points tell about the age of a site?

Projectile points changed over time in style and in size. These differences indicate when the point was made. The earliest points were larger and used on the end of spears and darts. As the bow and arrow began to replace the atlatl, points became smaller to accompany the smaller shaft of the arrow. A general guide to whether a point belonged to an atlatl dart or an arrow is the measurements of the artifact. If a point is wider than approximately one centimeter at the base of the point, then it was likely a dart. A measurement smaller than this would indicate an arrowhead.

Another method that can be used to date projectile points is by conducting radiocarbon testing on materials found near the point. Because radiocarbon dating can only be done on materials that were once alive, the actual point can not be tested. Materials found in the same layer of soil as the artifact are good clues as to when the point was being used. Blood residue found on points can be tested to see what the people were hunting at the time. If the result shows that they were hunting an Ice-Age camel, the point is clearly very old.

A timeline showing the difference in projectile points over time. The oldest point is on the top left, progressing to the most recent on the bottom right. The sizes became smaller as people shifted from dart points to arrowheads. Points are shown actual size.

a.   b.   c.

d.   e.   f.

Projectile Point Types

a. *Hell Gap point; Paleoindian era*
b. *Deception Creek point; Archaic era*
c. *McKean Lanceolate; Middle Plains Archaic era*
d. *Gatecliff Contracting Stem point; Archaic era*
e. *Rosegate point; Formative era*
f. *Desert Side-notched point, Protohistoric era*

Plate 538

THE PRIMITIVE ARTIST — PAVIOTSO

Historic photo by Edward Curtis

What is rock art?

Prehistoric rock art occurs on canyon walls, in rock shelters, and on boulders. Petroglyphs are created by etching or pecking into the rock face with a hard object. Rock paintings, often called pictographs, are created by painting a colored pigment onto the rock surface.

The subject matter of rock art included animals, human figures, abstract designs, and figures that seem to be religious in meaning. It is difficult to say exactly what the rock art means, but it is clear that it holds significance. Each panel is unique, not only to the culture but to the individuals who created it.

What does rock art tell us about prehistoric people?

Rock art offers insight into the people who created it. Rock was chosen as a medium because of its durability, creating images that would last. Images themselves are symbolic, representing something greater than themselves. Symbols are a way to communicate and transfer information. These panels would serve to express and reinforce group identities.

Some rock art seems to be a literal rendition of actual events such as animal migrations or hunts. Other pictures are abstract and geometric in style. These are the most difficult to guess at their meaning, as they might represent concepts, forces of nature, or a means of counting or tracking events. They may have had shamanistic meanings tied to rituals or visions. Themes such as tribal activities, religious and shamanistic images, fertility figures, and animals important to the people are recurring subjects.

Mythology and origin stories may have also been told through these images. They had rich symbology and mythical imagery that were unique to their group and culture.

The physical sites where the rock art is located seem to be significant. The same sites were added to over many years, showing that people were revisiting these locations. These rock art images would likely enhance the significance of these places.

It is impossible for archaeologists to say exactly what the rock art "means," but the very fact that it was created shows that the people had stories to tell that they valued enough to make permanent. Native Americans living today have many insightful interpretations into the meaning of the prehistoric rock art.

How did people move across the landscape through the course of the year?

The prehistoric people of northwest Colorado were mobile, changing their location with the seasons. The reason for their moving was that wild food resources are not abundant enough to permit living in only one place all year. The landscape in this area includes both mountains and river valleys, with elevations that vary from 4,500-14,000 feet. During different times of the year, great differences in temperature and available foods would be found between regions.

Early in spring, the first green shoots would be found at lower elevations, bringing the mule deer and other animals out to graze. Hunters would follow the herds to this area, and the fresh greens were enjoyed by the people as well. The group would pack their belongings and move up into the lower valleys to sites where they had lived the previous spring.

During the hot summers, the animals and people would move to higher elevations where plant food matured later because of cooler conditions. Summer was a time when mushrooms, leafy greens, and grass seeds could be collected. People would spend the winter in the mid-elevations, eating food they had stored and hunting wild game. This elevation also had the advantage of being centrally located to their spring and fall camps, making a shorter trip with all of their belongings.

Each year they would follow the same pattern, sometimes inhabiting the same site during the same time of year. If prehistoric people were like more recent hunters and gatherers, they made about nine residential moves a year, covering almost 230 miles. Their year was spread between several different home sites, moving when the food resources in an area were reduced to a level that made it worth the effort to move to another area with less-depleted resources.

How do archaeologists tell the season of a site's occupation?

The prehistoric people of northwestern Colorado were hunter-gatherers who moved between several different locations throughout the year. They followed game from higher to lower elevations as food resources got scarce. The elevation differences resulted in a variety of temperature and different environments that were more appealing at some times of year than others.

During the cold months, the tribes would live in the middle elevations to avoid the deeper snow and colder temperatures of the high country. In anticipation of a longer occupation, they constructed houses that offered more protection from the elements and were more permanent structures. These basin houses often had several hearths, showing that fires were used for cooking and heating indoors.

In contrast, the shelters they built during the summer were less substantial, sometimes as simple as sunshades made from branches or wikiups. These camps left less evidence for archaeologists to find as they were more likely to degrade over time. Locations of the sites offer a clue to the time of year it was occupied. During the hot season, people located their camps closer to water sources and in shady locations. In winter, proximity to water was less of a concern because of the availability of snow. These camps were placed in sunny locations that were protected from cold air draining out of the valleys.

Archaeologists are also able to get information about which season a site was occupied by identifying what types of food the people were eating at the time. Remains of eggshells are an example of a food that would have been collected and eaten early in the warm season. Another important indicator of a site occupied in spring are bones from fetal or juvenile animals. Seeds and berries can also offer information, but can sometimes be misleading because these foods could be stored for the cold months as well. During the winter months, people would have eaten more dried foods such as jerky and other foods that stored well.

Many of the sites that archaeologists are able to locate tend to be winter-occupied sites because of the more permanent nature of their construction.

Did prehistoric people have horses?

Native American people did not have horses until they were brought to North America by the Spaniards in the sixteenth century. Horses had been native to the Americas, but became extinct shortly after the last Ice Age. The Spaniards and other Europeans brought horses with their expeditions and raised horses in their settlements. Through trade and raids, Native Americans acquired horses. Some of the horses escaped and began to breed and increase their numbers in the wild. By the end of the eighteenth century, horses were common among tribes of the Plains.

The reintroduction of horses gave significant benefits to Native Americans. Riding horses was a much more effective way of hunting, especially for larger game. Tribes fully incorporated the use of horses into their societies and were able to extend their range into larger areas. This increased their contact with neighboring tribes, creating more opportunities for trade as well as warring raids. The tribes trained and used horses for riding and to carry packs or pull travois. The use of the horse had a profound impact on Native American culture and way of life.

Did they have pets?

Dogs were important animals to the prehistoric Native Americans. When people migrated to the North American continent approximately 13,000 years ago, they brought domesticated dogs with them. They were useful as "beasts of burden" and hunting companions. Archaeological evidence shows that prehistoric Native Americans were selectively breeding dogs that showed good hunting traits, such as speed, stamina, and strength. Dogs also helped people by hauling firewood, tents, and belongings on wooden frames called a travois.

Dog burial

Based on skeletal remains, these dogs were approximately the size of a Dalmatian and could probably carry around 10 pounds. Dogs were also eaten when food resources were low. Burials of canines have been found throughout the United States, many times in the same area where adults and children were buried. The importance of dogs to humans and the importance of their companionship are reflected in the caring way in which humans buried their dogs when they died.

What types of objects did they trade?

Trade was an important way for prehistoric people to acquire materials and objects that were not available in their region. They exchanged many things with other tribes. These items ranged from decorative items like beads, food, obsidian, and other types of rocks. Trade occurred when one group had more or different resources than another group.

Shell beads have been found in northwestern Colorado, almost 400 miles from where they originated. Artifacts made from shell found in this project include beads, pendants, part of a bracelet, and whole shells. This shows that prehistoric people in northwestern Colorado were part of a large trade network.

Obsidian is a volcanic rock that was sought after for its sharp edges when made into tools. Because there are slight mineral differences in the rock depending on where it was from, scientists are able to tell the location that the obsidian originated. Archaeologists found obsidian artifacts in the project area that came from as far away as 300 miles. These artifacts were made from obsidian that was traced to volcanic sources in what are now Idaho, Arizona, and New Mexico.

Another type of rock sought after for trade was steatite, or soapstone. It is a soft rock that is easy to carve. Prehistoric people used it to produce beads, pipes, pendants, and bowls.

The nearest source for steatite is in the Yellowstone area of Wyoming, making it likely that the people of this region were trading with bands from different regions for the stone.

Pottery was also traded between tribes. Although each group had their own pottery, stylistic differences between regions makes it possible to tell if a piece was from a different area. Pieces of pottery have been found outside of the areas where certain groups of people were known to have lived, indicating that the pottery was traded to other tribes.

After European peoples made contact with the Native Americans, overseas goods were traded. Fur traders made some of the first trades with the tribes, exchanging glass beads and metal objects for animal pelts. As more settlers and explorers came west, trade increased between the tribes and the Euroamericans.

Trading occurred between tribes throughout the year as groups traveled to other regions. Celebrations like marriages were also an opportunity for trade. Yearly rendezvous between groups of tribes also allowed for objects to be exchanged. Artifacts that were trade goods help to show how prehistoric tribes were interacting with groups from other areas.

Did the climate change through time?

Archaeologists are interested in climate changes throughout prehistory because of the ways that it affected humans who were living at the time. Hunter-gatherers were dependent upon the plants and animals in their environment for survival, and climate changes affected all living things in the region.

Many things affect the climate of the earth. Long-term climate changes are due to changes in the earth's orbit around the sun. These cycles last from 21,000 to 100,000 years and produce major changes in the earth's climate. Ice ages are an example of changes caused by these climate shifts.

Short-term climate changes can be caused by events such as volcanic eruptions spewing ash into the atmosphere, blocking sunlight from the earth's surface. The El Niño weather pattern is another example of short-term weather changes that affect people and their environment.

There are a number of ways that scientists can track climate changes thoughout history. One way is by looking at tree-rings. The changes in the environment affect a tree's growth, leaving thicker or thinner tree rings.

Another method is by studying ancient woodrat middens. These rodents collect virtually all types of vegetation within 150 feet of their nest and store it in rock overhangs and caves. These middens can be preserved for thousands of years, giving us an example of what types of plants were flourishing at different times.

Scientists can also study pollen and insects that are preserved within boggy marshlands called fens. Plant pollen shows what types of plants were thriving at certain times, which also gives an indication about rainfall amounts and how cool the temperatures were in the past.

The climate changed drastically over time in northwestern Colorado. Before 12,800 years ago, the highest elevations were covered by glaciers. The average temperatures were around 18 degrees Fahrenheit colder than current temperatures. People were beginning to live in this region around this time, hunting many Ice Age animals that are now extinct.

Two thousand years later, most of the glaciers were melted in Colorado by rapid global warming. The average temperatures were still around 10 degrees F cooler than present. The yearly rainfall was much higher during this time, but declined as the millennia passed. Around 7,000 years ago was a 200-year period of global cooling with more rain. Temperatures continued to increase each century, bringing the climate to the warmer, drier present-day conditions.

These climate changes affected what types of plants and animals could survive in the region. The Alpine tundra of the Ice Age was replaced with spruce forests, which then gave way to the pinyon trees and sagebrush that thrive here now. Many species of animals and plants became extinct after the Ice Age, affecting the prehistoric people who had depended upon them for food. People moved higher in elevations, following the animal herds that were seeking the cooler temperatures they were accustomed to. As the climate became warmer and drier, water became less readily available, shrinking the desirable habitats of many animals.

Climate changes affected prehistoric people by changing their environment and the plants and animals that lived in the region.

Shoshone man 1899

Were prehistoric people the same people as the historic Indian tribes?

People first came to the Americas around 13,000 years ago, possibly by crossing a land bridge that joined Siberia to Alaska. This area is now known as the Bering Strait. Humans migrated through the Americas, following game animals and spreading out through all of North and South America. The historic Indian tribes are the descendants of the prehistoric peoples that came before, although many changes happened after European contact. The tribes today have stories of the origins of their people and say that their ancestors have always been here.

Native American groups each had their own languages and customs, but they also met, traded, and intermarried with other groups. Once European settlers began to take over the West, the clash of cultures led to conflict. The government forced Native Americans onto reservations, and Euroamerican settlers changed the landscapes in which many tribes lived.

Whether the modern Indian tribes that were in northwestern Colorado when the Europeans arrived are the direct descendants of the prehistoric peoples represented in the archaeological record of the project area is a matter of debate. Some historic tribes moved widely across the continent, though often in response to conflict with Euroamerican culture.

Archaeologists have a difficult time tracing linkages between historic and prehistoric people, because so much of culture is not represented in the archaeological record. Languages and religious beliefs do not leave behind traces that are preserved in the ground, and past social organization and lifestyles can only be indirectly speculated. Prehistoric cultures were richer and more diverse than archaeologists can detect from the stone tools and fire pits common to their findings. The complex aspects of culture, most useful to understanding how groups organized and identified themselves, are lacking.

Five Ute women
1899

A.D. 2000	
	Protohistoric Era
A.D 1000	
	Formative Era
0 A.D/B.C	
1000 B.C	
2000 B.C.	
3000 B.C.	Archaic Era
4000 B.C.	
5000 B.C.	
6000 B.C.	
7000 B.C.	
8000 B.C.	
9000 B.C.	Paleoindian Era
10,000 B.C.	
11,000 B.C.	
Around 11,000 B.C., first indications of people living in Colorado	

Timelines of major archaeological eras in northwestern Colorado

Paeloindian Era

Approximately 11,500 and 6400 B.C.

Human occupation of northwestern Colorado began with the Paleoindian era. One of the characteristics of this era was hunting of big game, some types of which are now extinct. Plant gathering played a smaller, yet still important, role in their diet. Human populations were low and animal populations were high, making it possible for the prehistoric people to focus on big-game hunting. As the human populations increased and animal resources decreased, a shift in settlement occurred and plant gathering became more important. This marks the transition to the Archaic era.

Archaic Era

6400 and 200 B.C.

The Archaic era represents adaptations to essentially modern environments as the climate became warmer and drier. There was an increase of plant gathering for food, and a larger variety of plants was part of their diet. People used milling tools more, increasing the amount of seeds and grains in their diet. There was a shift in hunting from primarily big game towards hunting many different types of animals. People were relatively mobile, moving through the environment during different times of year.

Formative Era

200 B.C. and A.D. 1300

The Formative era refers to the time when corn was introduced into some portions of western Colorado. Not all people were farming corn at this time, as the growing seasons in some areas were too short for corn, beans, and squash. Gathering was still an important source of food. People began making pottery during this era. The prehistoric people were still relatively mobile but settled in more specific territories as the populations grew. Larger populations meant more competition for food and shelter, and groups attached themselves to territories to protect their resources.

Protohistoric Era

A.D. 1300 and A.D. 1770

The Protohistoric era lasts from the end of the Formative era until the final expulsion of Native Americans to the existing reservations in the late nineteenth century. This era is the time where European settlers made contact with the Native Americans and horses were reintroduced to the Americas. Historic and archaeological data indicate that the Ute and the Shoshone were the primary indigenous occupants of Northwestern Colorado during the Protohistoric era. The start of the Historic period marked the end of the Protohistoric era.

A knife made from tiger chert

Artifacts found in northwestern Colorado.

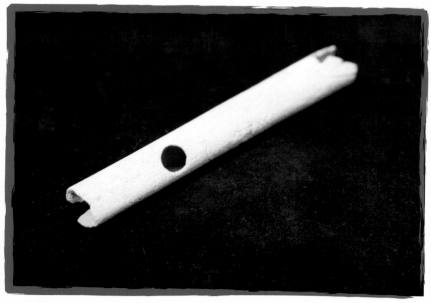

Flute carved from bone

Why is it important to leave artifacts in place?

Removing artifacts without using proper scientific methods destroys evidence that is used to interpret a site. It is important to know where artifacts were located and what artifacts were associated with one another. The removal of artifacts results in the destruction of archaeological sites and of contextual information that is essential to understanding the archaeological record. Even when people are just collecting arrowheads on hikes, information about a site is lost forever.

An archaeologist records all manner of details surrounding an artifact and its environment. The location of the artifact, depth at which it is buried, and context in which it is found all give insight into what prehistoric people were doing. An artifact removed from its setting has lost its scientific value. Detailed descriptions are crucial if cultural patterns are to be discovered, tested, and compared. The true value of artifacts is in their original context, not the objects themselves.

How can I find out more about the region's archaeology?

The following books have lots of great information about the archaeology and prehistoric people of this region.

Ancient Peoples of the Great Basin and Colorado Plateau. by Steven R. Simms, 2008, Left Coast Press, Walnut Creek, California.

The Archaeology of Colorado. by E. Steve Cassells, 1997, Johnson Books, Boulder Colorado.

The People of the Red Earth. by Sally Crum. 1996, Ancient City Press, Santa Fe, New Mexico.

The Colorado Historical Society in Denver, Colorado is also a good resource. The Colorado History Museum is located at 1300 Broadway, Denver, Colorado 80203.
Website: www.coloradohistory.org

Photo Credits

Except as noted, photographs are by Marlise Reed and Alpine Archaeological Consultant, Inc.

Curtis, Edward S.
2001 *'The North American Indian': the Photographic Images.*
http://hdl.loc.gov/loc.award/iencurt.cp15026; page 35, 36.
Northwestern University Library

Curtis, Edward S.
2001 *'The North American Indian': the Photographic Images.*
http://hdl.loc.gov/loc.award/iencurt.cp15029; pages 39, 48, 56
Northwestern University Library

Curtis, Edward S.
2001 *'The North American Indian': the Photographic Images.*
http:hdl.loc.gov/loc.award/iencurt.cp01038; pages 65, 67

Jack Woody/US Fish and Wildlife Service/ antelope; page 13

Denver Public Library, Western History Department,
http://photoswest.org/cgibin/imager?10032502+X-32502
Shoshone man X-32502; page 36

Metcalf Archaeological Consultants, projectile points; page 47

Jeremy Matlock, page 75

Illustrations

Marlise Reed: pages 10, 15, 16, 25, 29, 30, 32, 36, 40, 58

Eric Carlson: pages 19, 22, 23, 31

Sandra Combs: pages 20, 68

Stephanie Dudash: page 3

Public domain illustration: page 66

References

Do archaeologists dig dinosaurs? Adapted from essay by Jason Fancher

Illustration inspired by design on ShovelBums.org; page 16

About the Author

Photo by Jeremy Matlock

Marlise Reed earned a B.A. in Studio Arts at the University of Colorado in Boulder. She has worked as a photographer and painter since college. Her photos have been published in the book *Bolivia Querida*. Since returning from Bolivia where she taught beekeeping as a Peace Corps volunteer, she has been working as a graphic designer. A lifelong resident of Colorado, she enjoys yoga and hiking in the mountains.